Anna Del Conte's Italian Kitchen

I Risotti

AND OTHER ITALIAN RICE DISHES

ILLUSTRATED BY FLO BAYLEY

PAVILION

First published in Great Britain in 1993 by
PAVILION BOOKS LIMITED
26 Upper Ground, London SE1 9PD

A CIP catalogue record for this book is
available from the British Library

ISBN 1 85793 0339

Printed and bound in Italy by New Interlitho

2 4 6 8 10 9 7 5 3 1

This book may be ordered by post direct from
the publisher. Please contact the Marketing
Department. But try your bookshop first.

CONTENTS

RISOTTI

Risotto is a relative newcomer to the Italian culinary scene, where most dishes can trace their origins back to the Renaissance, if not to Roman times. It was only during the nineteenth century that risotto became popular in the northern regions of Italy – Piedmont, Lombardy and Veneto – where the rice was cultivated, as indeed it still is.

A genuine risotto, for all its apparent simplicity, is a challenge to most cooks. Although there are certain rules to observe, the feel of making a good risotto can only be learnt with practice. The first essential is to use top quality ingredients. Secondly, one must remember that risotto is prepared according to a well-defined method. It is not just a mixture of rice and other ingredients, and it is certainly not, as some people have believed, a dish that Italians make from an assortment of leftovers. Rice is often the only ingredient, apart from flavourings. When there are other ingredients they are almost always cooked with the rice, so as to allow the flavours to combine and fuse.

The rice must be medium-grain white rice, which absorbs the liquid in which it cooks and which swells up without breaking or becoming mushy. Only two types of rice are suitable for making risotto: superfino and fino. Arborio, which is widely available, is the most popular variety of superfino rice and is suitable for all risotti. It has large plump grains with a delicious nutty taste when cooked. Carnaroli, a new superfino variety, is produced in relatively small quantities. It keeps its firm consistency, while its starch dissolves deliciously during the cooking. Vialone Nano, a fino rice, has a shorter, stubbier grain containing starch of a kind that does not soften easily in the cooking. It is my favourite rice for vegetable risotti. Vialone Nano cooks more quickly than

Arborio – 15 minutes as opposed to 20 minutes for Arborio. Both Carnaroli and Vialone Nano can be found in specialist Italian shops. In most of the recipes I have specified the best variety of rice to use, bearing in mind availability.

The choice of saucepan is crucial to the success of the dish. The pan must be wide, heavy-bottomed and large enough to contain the rice when it has finished cooking, by which time it will have increased its volume by nearly three times. Ideally it should also be round-bottomed, to prevent the rice from sticking in the corners.

The quality of the stock is also very important. It should be a good, but light, meat stock, made with a piece of veal, some beef, one or two pieces of chicken and very few bones, all flavoured with vegetables, herbs and seasonings. Pork and lamb are never used for this kind of stock. Vegetable stock is particularly suitable for a vegetable or fish risotto; for the latter a light fish stock is also good. If you have not got any stock already prepared, use good quality meat stock cubes; there are some on the market that do not contain monosodium glutamate.

Good quality Italian rice takes about 15–20 minutes to cook, according to the variety. At the end of the cooking the rice should be *al dente* – firm but tender without a chalky centre – and the risotto should have a creamy consistency.

You will find here recipes for 12 risotti, many with vegetables, others with fish and with meat. These last are more nourishing and are definitely main course dishes, while the lighter risotti with vegetables can be the start, *all'Italiana*, of any dinner party.

Risotto should be eaten as soon as it is done, but if you do not like to cook when your guests have already arrived, you can make a *timballo* instead, and accompany it with a suitable sauce if you wish. For this, keep the risotto slightly undercooked, being careful to add the stock very gradually at the end of the cooking or the rice will be too liquid when it is ready. Spread the risotto out on a large dish and leave it to cool. When it is cold, spoon it into a ring mould that has been generously buttered and sprinkled with dried breadcrumbs.

Set the mould in a bain-marie and bake in the oven heated to 220°C/425°F/Gas Mark 7 for about 20 minutes. Loosen the risotto all round the mould with a palette knife. Place a large round platter over it and turn the whole thing upside-down. Give the mould a few taps on the top, shake the platter and mould vigorously and lift the mould away. If some of the risotto sticks to the mould, remove it and patch the shape up neatly. Nobody will notice, especially if you place some basil or parsley over it.

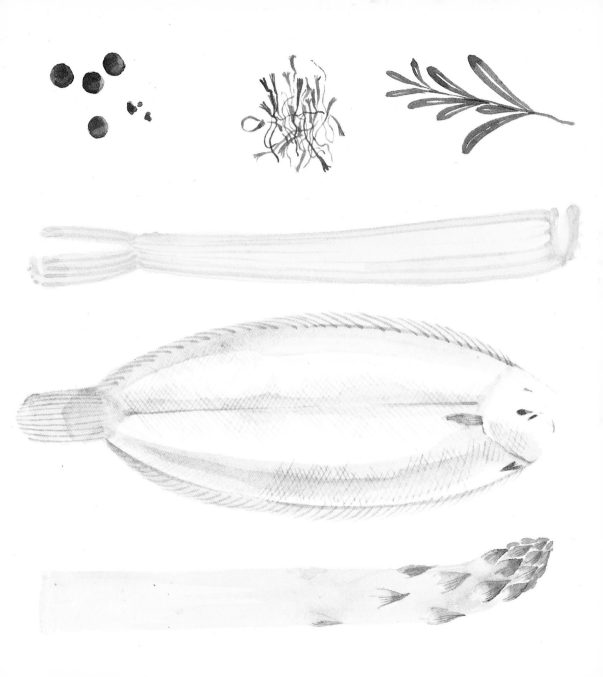

RISOTTO IN BIANCO

RISOTTO WITH PARMESAN

Serves 4–5 as a first course or as an accompaniment

1.5l/2½pt light meat stock
2 shallots or 1 small onion, very finely chopped
60g/2oz unsalted butter
350g/¾lb Italian rice, preferably Carnaroli or Arborio
60g/2oz Parmesan, freshly grated
salt and freshly ground black pepper

This is the basic risotto and, as such, the purest of any. It is the one that, during the truffle season, is crowned with slivers of white truffle. In Italy it is mostly eaten by itself, but you can serve it as an accompaniment to meat.

1 Bring the stock to a gentle simmer (keep it simmering all through the cooking of the rice).

2 Meanwhile, put the shallots or onion in a heavy-bottomed saucepan with half the butter. Sauté for about 7 minutes or until translucent and soft.

3 Add the rice and stir until well coated with the butter. Sauté, stirring constantly with a wooden spoon, until the grains become partly translucent and the rice begins to stick to the bottom of the pan.

4 Now pour over about 150ml/¼pt of the simmering stock. Stir very thoroughly and cook until the rice has absorbed nearly all the stock, then add another ladleful. Continue to add stock gradually, and in small quantities, so that the rice always cooks in liquid but is never drowned by it. Stir constantly at first; after that you need to stir frequently but not all the time. In Milan we say that a good risotto should just catch at the bottom. The heat should be moderate, so as to keep the rice at a steady and lively simmer. If you run out of stock before the rice is cooked, add some boiling water.

5 When the rice is *al dente* (good rice takes at least 15 minutes), draw the pan off the heat. Add the rest of the butter, cut into small pieces, the Parmesan and seasoning to taste and put the lid firmly on the pan. Leave for 1 minute, until the butter and Parmesan have melted, and then give the risotto a vigorous stir. Serve at once, with more Parmesan handed separately in a bowl.

This dish can easily become a risotto with dried porcini. Pour 150ml/$\frac{1}{4}$pt of very hot water over 30g/1oz of dried porcini. Leave for 30 minutes and then lift them out and rinse under cold water. Dry well. Chop them finely and add them to the shallots or onion. Sauté them for 1 minute before you add the rice, then proceed according to the recipe above. Filter the liquid in which the porcini have soaked through a sieve lined with muslin and add it to the rice while it is cooking.

RISOTTO AL LIMONE

RISOTTO WITH LEMON

Serves 4 as a first course or 3
as a main course

1.25l/2pt home-made light meat
stock or vegetable stock
60g/2oz unsalted butter
1 tbsp olive oil
2 shallots, very finely chopped
1 celery stick, very finely
chopped
300g/10oz Italian rice,
preferably Arborio
½ unwaxed lemon
5 or 6 fresh sage leaves
leaves from a small sprig of
fresh rosemary
1 egg yolk
4 tbsp freshly grated Parmesan
4 tbsp double cream
salt and freshly ground
black pepper

This recipe was in my book, *Secrets from an Italian Kitchen*.
Friends and reviewers alike have all said they found it one
of the best risotti ever, which is why I feel no qualms about
repeating it here.

1 Bring the stock to a gentle simmer (keep it simmering all
through the cooking of the rice).

2 Heat half the butter, the oil, shallots and celery in a heavy
bottomed saucepan and sauté until the *soffritto* – frying mixture –
of shallot and celery is softened (about 7 minutes). Mix in the
rice and continue to sauté, stirring, until the rice is well coated
with the fats and is partly translucent.

3 Pour over about 150ml/¼pt of the simmering stock. Stir very
thoroughly and cook until the rice has absorbed nearly all of the
stock, still stirring. Add another ladleful of simmering stock, and
continue in this manner until the rice is ready. You may not need
all the stock. Good quality Italian rice for risotto takes 15–20
minutes to cook.

4 Meanwhile, thinly pare the zest from the lemon half and chop
it with the herbs. Mix into the rice halfway through the cooking.

5 Squeeze the half lemon into a small bowl and combine it with
the egg yolk, Parmesan, cream, a little salt and a very generous
grinding of black pepper. Mix well with a fork.

6 When the rice is *al dente*, draw the pan off the heat and stir in
the egg and cream mixture and the remaining butter. Cover the
pan and leave to rest for 2 minutes or so. Then give the risotto an
energetic stir, transfer to a heated dish or bowl and serve at once,
with more grated Parmesan in a little bowl if you wish.

RISOTTO ALLA MILANESE
RISOTTO WITH SAFFRON

Serves 4–5 as a first course or
as an accompaniment

1.5l/2½pt home-made light
meat stock
1 small onion, very finely
chopped
75g/2½oz unsalted butter
350g/¾lb Italian rice, preferably
Carnaroli
180ml/6fl oz good red wine
½ tsp powdered saffron or saffron
strands crushed to a powder
salt and freshly ground
black pepper
75g/2½oz Parmesan,
freshly grated

S ome Italians have queried the use of red wine instead of white
in this recipe. My answer is that not only in my own family –
Milanese for generations – but in some very authoritative books
the wine suggested is red. Other recipes do not include any wine,
but add some cream or milk at the end. The choice is yours.

As for the saffron, the strands are definitely more reliable than
the powder, but they must be added earlier in the cooking so as
to dissolve well, thus losing some flavour during the cooking.

This is the risotto traditionally served with Ossobuco and with
Costolette alla Milanese, breaded veal cutlets.

1 Bring the stock to simmering point (keep it at a very low simmer
all through the cooking of the rice).
2 Put the onion and 60g/2oz of the butter in a heavy-bottomed
saucepan and sauté until soft and translucent. Add the rice and
stir until well coated with fat. Sauté until the rice is partly
translucent. Pour in the wine and boil for 1 minute, stirring
constantly, and then pour in 150ml/¼pt of the simmering stock.
Cook until nearly all the stock has been absorbed and then add
another ladleful of the simmering stock. Continue cooking and
adding small quantities of stock, while keeping the risotto at a
steady lively simmer all the time. If you finish the stock before
the rice is properly cooked, add a little boiling water.
3 About halfway through the cooking (good rice takes about 15–
20 minutes to cook), add the saffron dissolved in a little stock.
When the rice is *al dente*, taste and adjust the seasoning.
4 Draw the pan off the heat and mix in the rest of the butter and
4 tbsp of the Parmesan. Put the lid on and leave for 1 minute or

so. When the butter and the Parmesan have melted, give the risotto a vigorous stir and transfer to a heated dish. Serve immediately, with the rest of the cheese handed round separately.

RISOTTO AL POMODORO
RISOTTO WITH TOMATOES

The match of risotto with tomatoes is a modern one, but it is so good that I am sure it will become a classic. This risotto does not contain any butter. It is very light and fresh, and it is very good, if not better, cold.

Serves 4 as a first course or 3 as a main course

700g/1½lb ripe tomatoes, peeled
7 tbsp extra virgin olive oil
3 or 4 garlic cloves, thickly sliced
a good handful of fresh basil leaves, torn into pieces
1.25l/2pt vegetable stock
300g/10oz Italian rice, preferably Carnaroli
salt and freshly ground black pepper

1 Cut the peeled tomatoes in half. Squeeze out and discard some of the seeds. Chop the tomatoes coarsely and put them in a heavy-bottomed saucepan large enough to hold the rice later. Remember that the rice will be nearly three times its original volume by the end of the cooking.

2 Add 4 tbsp of the oil to the pan, then add the garlic and half the basil. Cook briskly for 1–2 minutes, stirring.

3 Meanwhile, bring the stock to a simmer (keep it simmering very gently all through the making of the risotto).

4 Add the rice to the pan with the tomatoes and cook for about 2 minutes, stirring constantly.

5 Pour over a ladleful of simmering stock and continue cooking, adding more stock little by little until the rice is *al dente*. If you want to serve the risotto cold, remove it from the heat when the rice is slightly underdone; it finishes cooking as it cools.

6 Add salt and pepper to taste and mix in the rest of the oil. Transfer to a serving dish and sprinkle the remaining basil leaves on the top. If you serve the risotto cold, fluff it up with a fork before bringing it to the table.

RISOTTO AL FINOCCHIO
RISOTTO WITH FENNEL

Serves 4–5 as a first course or
3–4 as a main course

2 fennel bulbs, about 600g/1¼lb
1 tbsp olive oil
60g/2oz unsalted butter
1 small onion, finely chopped
1 celery stick, finely chopped
1.25l/2pt vegetable stock
salt and freshly ground
black pepper
300g/10oz Italian rice,
preferably Vialone Nano
6 tbsp dry white wine
4 tbsp double cream
50g/1¾oz Parmesan,
freshly grated

Vegetable risotti are one of the great strengths of Venetian cooking. Of all of them, this fennel risotto is my favourite, especially when I can get hold of fennel that is full of flavour and not 'the commercial variety grown in Italy for export which is beautiful but dumb' as the late Jane Grigson so aptly put it in her splendid *Vegetable Book*.

1 Cut off and discard the fennel stalks, but keep some of the feathery green foliage. Remove any bruised outer leaves and then cut the bulbs lengthwise in half. Slice the halves very finely across. Wash thoroughly and drain.

2 Put the oil, half the butter, the onion and celery in a smallish sauté pan. Sauté until the vegetables are pale gold. Add the sliced fennel and stir it over and over to let it take up the flavour. Add about 4 tbsp of the stock and cover the pan. Cook, stirring occasionally, for about 20 minutes or until the fennel is very soft. Mash it with a fork to a purée over high heat, so that the excess liquid evaporates. Add salt to taste.

3 Bring the remaining stock to a gentle simmer (keep it simmering all through the cooking of the rice).

4 Heat the remaining butter in a heavy-bottomed saucepan. When the butter foam begins to subside, mix in the rice and stir to coat the grains thoroughly. Sauté for a couple of minutes until the rice is partly translucent. Turn the heat up and add the wine. Let it bubble away, stirring the rice constantly.

5 Now begin to add the simmering stock a ladleful at a time. When nearly all of the first ladleful has been absorbed, add another, always stirring the rice. If you run out of stock before the rice is done, add some boiling water and continue the cooking.

6 Halfway through the cooking of the rice, stir in the mashed fennel with all the cooking juices.

7 When the rice is *al dente*, draw the pan from the heat and add the cream, Parmesan and a generous grinding of pepper. Mix everything well together. Transfer to a heated dish, scatter the reserved fennel foliage, previously snipped, over the top and serve at once.

RISOTTO AL PEPERONE

RISOTTO WITH PEPPERS

Serves 4 as a first course or 3
as a main course

6 tbsp extra virgin olive oil
2 garlic cloves, sliced
3 tbsp chopped fresh parsley
4 tomatoes, peeled, seeded
and chopped
2 large peppers, preferably
1 yellow and 1 red
1.25l/2pt vegetable stock
300g/10oz Italian rice,
preferably Arborio or
Vialone Nano
4 pinches of chilli powder
salt and freshly ground
black pepper
12 fresh basil leaves

Risotto, the staple of northern Italy, used never to be made with olive oil, the cooking fat of the south. But a few modern risotti are now very successfully made with oil, and with ingredients, in this case peppers, whose ideal dressing is oil.

This is my adaptation of a traditional risotto from Voghera, a town in south-west Lombardy that is famous for its peppers.

1 Heat 4 tbsp of the oil in a heavy-bottomed saucepan with the garlic and parsley. When the garlic and parsley begin to sizzle, add the chopped tomatoes and cook for 5 minutes, stirring frequently.

2 Meanwhile wash and dry the peppers. Peel them, using a swivel-headed vegetable peeler. You should 'saw' from side to side with it as you peel, rather than sliding it straight down the pepper. If you find them difficult to peel, leave the skin on. Discard the cores, seeds and white ribs, and cut the peppers into small cubes.

3 Add the peppers to the pan and cook for 10 minutes, stirring frequently.

4 Meanwhile, bring the stock to a simmer in another pan. (Keep it just simmering all through the cooking). Add the rice to the tomato and pepper mixture and stir very well, letting it absorb the juices. After about 1–2 minutes, begin to add the simmering stock by the ladleful. Wait to add each subsequent ladleful until the previous one has nearly all been absorbed.

5 When the rice is *al dente*, about 18 minutes, add the chilli powder and salt and pepper to taste. Draw the pan off the heat and stir in the remaining 2 tbsp of oil. Transfer to a heated deep serving dish, sprinkle with the basil leaves and serve at once.

RISOTTO ALLA PAESANA

— RISOTTO WITH VEGETABLES —

Thi his lovely fresh risotto is best made in the spring, when the new peas and asparagus are in season. The vegetables can be varied: you can put in a little celery and carrot when there is no asparagus; French beans are suitable too. Try to match the flavours of the vegetables so as not to have a strident note.

1 Cook the fresh peas in lightly salted boiling water until just tender. Meanwhile, trim and wash the asparagus and cook them in boiling salted water until *al dente*. Drain and cut the tender part of the spears into small pieces. (Reserve the rest for a soup or a mousse.) Blanch the courgette for 2–3 minutes, then drain and cut into small cubes. Cut the tomatoes in half, squeeze out the seeds and then cut into short strips.

2 Put half the oil, the parsley and garlic in a sauté pan and sauté for 1 minute. Stir in all the vegetables, season lightly with salt and sauté over low heat for 2 minutes for them to take the flavour of the *soffritto* – the fried mixture. Set aside.

3 Heat the stock in a saucepan until just simmering (keep it simmering all through the cooking of the rice).

4 Put the rest of the oil and half the butter in a heavy-bottomed saucepan. Add the shallots and sauté until tender. Add the rice and stir to coat with the fats, then cook for 2 minutes or until partly translucent. Splash with the wine and boil rapidly to evaporate, stirring constantly. Add a ladleful of simmering stock and let the rice absorb it while you stir constantly. Continue to add the stock gradually, stirring frequently, until the rice is *al dente*. (This will take about 15 to 20 minutes, according to the quality of the rice.)

5 Halfway through the cooking, stir in the vegetables with all their cooking juices. Season with pepper; taste to check the salt.

Serves 4 as a first course or 3 as a main course

100g/3½oz podded fresh peas
225g/½lb asparagus
100g/3½oz courgette
225g/½lb ripe firm tomatoes, peeled, Italian canned or plum tomatoes, drained
4 tbsp extra virgin olive oil
a bunch of fresh parsley, chopped
1 garlic clove, chopped
salt and freshly ground black pepper
1.25l/2pt chicken or vegetable stock
30g/1oz unsalted butter
2 shallots, chopped
250g/9oz Italian rice, preferably Vialone Nano
5 tbsp dry white wine
45g/1½oz Parmesan, freshly grated
12 fresh basil leaves, torn into pieces

6 When the rice is done, draw the pan off the heat and add the rest of the butter, cut into small pieces, and the Parmesan. Place the lid tightly on the pan and allow to stand for a couple of minutes. Then stir vigorously and transfer to a heated dish. Garnish with the basil leaves and serve at once.

RISOTTO COI PEOCI

RISOTTO WITH MUSSELS

Serves 4 as a first course or 3 as a main course

1.8kg/4lb mussels
300ml/½pt dry white wine
4 tbsp chopped fresh parsley, preferably flat-leaf
6 tbsp olive oil
3 shallots or 1 medium onion, very finely chopped
salt and freshly ground black pepper
1l/1¾pt light fish or vegetable stock
1 celery stick, with the leaves if possible
1 garlic clove
½ dried chilli, crumbled
300g/10oz Italian rice, preferably Arborio or Vialone Nano

I have always found a risotto with mussels to be rather unsatisfactory, because you either have only risotto in your mouth, albeit fish tasting, or else a large mussel. So one day I came up with the idea of chopping up most of the mussels so that morsels of them could be enjoyed in each mouthful. This is the recipe I developed and it works very well.

1 First clean the mussels. Scrape off the barnacles, tug off the beard and scrub thoroughly with a stiff brush under running water. Throw away any mussel that remains open after you have tapped it on a hard surface; this means it's dead.

2 Put the wine in a large sauté pan, add the mussels and cover the pan. Cook over high heat until the mussels are open, which will only take 3–4 minutes. Shake the pan every now and then.

3 As soon as the mussels are open, remove the meat from the shells and discard the shells. Strain the cooking liquid through a sieve lined with muslin, pouring it slowly and gently so that the sand will be left at the bottom of the pan.

4 Set aside a dozen of the nicest mussels; chop the rest and put in a bowl. Mix in the parsley.

5 Pour the oil into a heavy-bottomed saucepan. Add the shallots or onion and a pinch of salt and sauté until the shallot is soft and just beginning to colour.

6 In another saucepan, heat the stock to simmering point (keep it just simmering all through the cooking of the rice).

7 Meanwhile, chop the celery and garlic together. Add to the shallot with the chilli. Sauté for a further minute or so. Now add the rice and stir to coat with oil, then cook it for a couple of minutes until partly translucent. Pour over the mussel liquid and stir well. When the liquid has been absorbed add the simmering stock, one ladleful at a time. Stir constantly at first. When the rice is nearly cooked, mix in the chopped mussels, then continue cooking until *al dente*.

8 Season with salt, if necessary, and pepper. Transfer to a heated dish and garnish with the reserved whole mussels.

RISOTTO CON LE ANIMELLE
—— RISOTTO WITH SWEETBREADS ——

In restaurants, sweetbreads are often accompanied by boiled rice. That rather boring presentation has, however, led me to devise this dish, where the winey-syrupy sweetbreads are combined with a classic *risotto in bianco*.

During the truffle season a small white truffle shaved over the top of the risotto makes the dish truly sensational.

1 Soak the sweetbreads in cold water for at least 1 hour. Rinse them and put them in a pan with half lemon and 1 tsp of salt. Cover with fresh cold water and bring to the boil. Boil for 2 minutes. Drain well, plunge into cold water and drain again.

Remove all fat and the white tubes, as well as the hard bits. Put the sweetbreads between two plates with a weight on top to squeeze out all excess liquid. Dry them and cut them into morsels.

2 Heat the stock to simmering (keep it simmering all through the cooking of the risotto).

3 Melt half the butter in a heavy-bottomed saucepan. Add the shallots, 4 of the sage leaves and a pinch of salt and cook until the shallots are soft and translucent.

4 Add the rice and stir to coat with butter, then sauté for 2 to 3 minutes until partly translucent. Pour in the wine and boil for a minute or two until it has evaporated, stirring constantly. Now begin to add simmering stock, little by little, in the usual way. Do not add too much at one time or the risotto will not cook properly. Keep the heat lively and constant.

5 Meanwhile, melt half the remaining butter in a sauté or frying pan. Add the rest of the sage leaves. When the sage begins to sizzle, slide in the sweetbreads and sauté for 2 minutes, turning them over to brown on all sides. Add the Marsala to the pan and let it bubble away on a slow heat. Cook for 7–8 minutes, stirring occasionally.

6 When the rice is nearly done, pour the sweetbreads and all the juices into the risotto pan. Stir thoroughly. Taste and adjust the seasoning, and finish cooking the risotto.

7 When the rice is *al dente*, draw the pan off the heat. Add the remaining butter and a couple of spoonsful of the Parmesan. Cover the pan tightly and let the butter melt for a minute or so, then stir the risotto gently but thoroughly. Transfer to a heated dish and serve at once, handing round the rest of the Parmesan in a bowl.

Serves 4 as a main course

450g/1lb lamb sweetbreads
$\frac{1}{2}$ lemon
salt and freshly ground black pepper
1.25l/2pt light meat stock
120g/4oz unsalted butter
2 shallots, finely chopped
about 8 fresh sage leaves, snipped
300g/10oz Italian rice, preferably Arborio
6 tbsp dry white wine
4 tbsp Marsala (Madeira or port can also be used)
75g/2$\frac{1}{2}$oz Parmesan, freshly grated

RISOTTO CON LE SOGLIOLE
RISOTTO WITH DOVER SOLE

Serves 4 as a main course

75g/2½oz unsalted butter
2 tbsp very finely chopped shallot
salt and freshly ground black pepper
1.25l/2pt light fish stock
350g/¾lb Italian rice, preferably Carnaroli
120ml/4fl oz dry white wine
2 tbsp chopped fresh dill
350g/¾lb skinless Dover sole fillets
4 tbsp freshly grated Parmesan

It might seem extravagant to use Dover sole in a humble dish such as a risotto, but I assure you that it is necessary. You only need a small amount of Dover sole, and it does make a great difference to the dish. The delicacy and firm texture of the fish is in perfect harmony with the soft creaminess of the risotto; none of the other ingredients disturbs this happy balance of flavours.

1 Heat 60g/2oz of the butter and the shallot in a heavy-bottomed saucepan. Add a pinch of salt and sauté until the shallot is soft and translucent.

2 Meanwhile, heat the fish stock in another saucepan to simmering (keep it at the lowest simmer all through the cooking of the risotto).

3 Add the rice to the shallot and stir to coat with butter, then sauté for a minute or so until partly translucent. Splash with wine and let it bubble away, stirring constantly.

4 Add about 150ml/¼pt of simmering stock, stir well and let the rice absorb the liquid. Continue adding stock little by little until the rice is nearly done, then mix in half of the dill and continue the cooking.

5 Meanwhile, heat the remaining butter in a non-stick frying pan. Cut the fish fillets in half, across. Slide them into the butter and sauté for 3 minutes. Turn them over and sauté for a further minute. Sprinkle with salt and pepper.

6 When the rice is *al dente*, mix in the Parmesan and the juices from the fish fillets. Turn into a heated dish. Place the fish fillets neatly over the top and sprinkle with the remaining dill. Serve immediately.

RISOTTO ALLA SCOZZESE
RISOTTO WITH SMOKED SALMON AND
WHISKY

Serves 4 as a first course or 3
as a main course

60g/2oz unsalted butter
4 tbsp finely chopped shallot
salt
1.25l/2 pt vegetable or light
chicken stock
300g/10oz Italian rice,
preferably Carnaroli
4 tbsp Scotch whisky
225g/½lb smoked salmon,
cut into 2cm/¾in pieces
5 tbsp double cream
2 tbsp chopped fresh dill
cayenne pepper
freshly grated Parmesan,
to serve

I love smoked salmon and, like most Italians, am not averse to an occasional glass of whisky. So here I have combined these two very Scottish ingredients with a favourite dish from my home country. This match with a Lombard risotto is particularly successful. The Parmesan is not necessary, but I think its flavour goes well with that of the smoked salmon.

1 Put the butter in a large, heavy-bottomed saucepan. Add the chopped shallot and a pinch of salt; this will release the moisture from the shallot thus preventing it from browning. Sauté until soft and translucent, about 7 minutes.

2 Meanwhile, in another saucepan heat the stock to simmering point (keep it simmering all through the cooking of the rice).

3 Add the rice to the shallot and stir to coat with butter, then cook for a couple of minutes, stirring constantly, until partly translucent. Add the whisky and let it bubble away, stirring constantly. Add a ladleful of simmering stock and cook the rice on a lively heat, adding a ladleful of stock whenever the rice begins to get dry.

4 When the rice is *al dente*, add the smoked salmon, cream, dill and cayenne pepper to taste. Mix thoroughly and check the salt before you transfer this delicious risotto to a heated dish. Serve at once, handing the cheese separately in a bowl for those who want it.

RISOTTO CON LA SALSICCIA
RISOTTO WITH SAUSAGE

Some recipes for this dish, originally from Monza (now a suburb of Milan) suggest cutting the sausage in chunks and cooking it separately. In this case the sausage is also served separately and is added to the risotto by each diner. I find this version more suitable if I am serving the risotto as a main course. Here, however, the recipe is for a real risotto, the sausage being added to the rice about 10 minutes before the rice is ready, so that the flavours of the two ingredients will blend thoroughly.

You need good 100% pure pork sausage.

Serves 4 as a first course or 3 as a main course

350g/¾lb luganega sausage or other pure pork, coarse-grained, continental sausage
2 tbsp olive oil
1 sprig of fresh sage
150ml/¼pt full-bodied red wine, such as Barbera
1.25l/2pt light meat stock
45g/1½oz unsalted butter
2 or 3 shallots, depending on size, finely chopped
300g/10oz Italian rice, preferably Arborio or Carnaroli
salt and freshly ground black pepper
freshly grated Parmesan, to serve (optional)

1 Skin the sausage and crumble it. Heat 1 tbsp of oil and the sage in a non-stick frying pan. Add the sausage and fry briskly for 5 minutes, stirring constantly. Pour over the wine, bring to the boil and cook for about 5 minutes, only enough for the sausage meat to lose its raw colour.

2 While the sausage is cooking bring the stock to a simmer (keep it just simmering all through the cooking of the rice).

3 Heat butter and remaining oil in a heavy-bottomed saucepan. Add the shallots and fry gently until soft and translucent – about 7 minutes.

4 Add the rice to the shallot *soffritto* and cook for 1–2 minutes, stirring constantly, until the grains are partly translucent.

5 Add the simmering stock a ladleful at a time. Wait to add another ladleful until the previous one has nearly all been absorbed.

6 Ten minutes after you start adding the stock, add the sausage and its juice to the rice. Stir well and continue cooking until the rice is *al dente*. Check the seasoning and serve at once, with the Parmesan handed round separately if you wish.

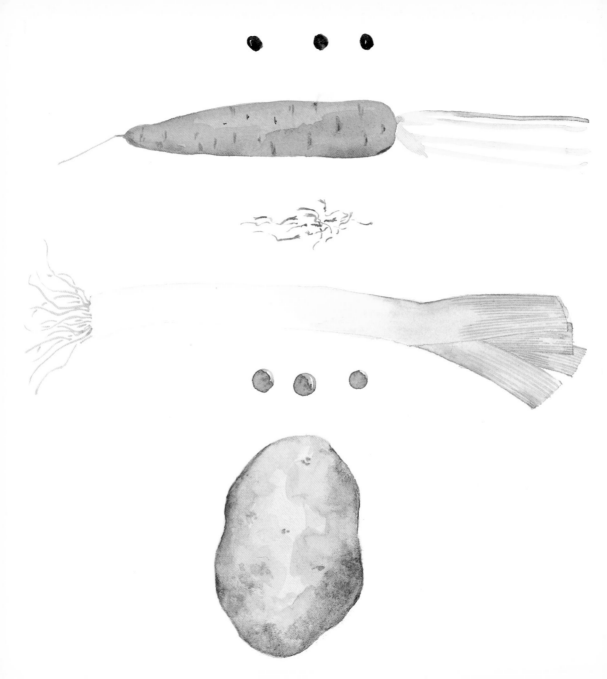

TIMBALLI E PASTICCI DI RISO

MOULDED AND BAKED RICE DISHES

I have included three recipes for this type of rice preparation. There are two elegant moulded dishes and a rice, potato and mussel pie of peasant origin but of great gastronomic merit. All three are particularly suited to dinner parties, since they can be made in advance and then baked in the oven. They are dishes that need a more experienced cook, able to judge the exact cooking time of the different ingredients, and, in the case of the moulded dishes, able to shape and unmould the rice. A good point, however, is that cooked rice is very malleable. Should you find yourself with a timballo *tombé*, you can reshape the rice with your hands and nobody will know. The pie is easy as regards presentation, but requires knowledge in the timing.

SFORMATO DI RISOTTO E PORRI CON LA SALSA DI COZZE

MOULDED LEEK RISOTTO WITH MUSSEL
SAUCE

**Serves 6 as a first course or 4
as a main course**

1kg/2¼lb mussels
1 tbsp olive oil
2 garlic cloves
1 thick slice of lemon
350g/¾lb leeks
1.25/2pt vegetable stock
120g/4oz unsalted butter
450g/1lb Italian rice, preferably
Vialone Nano
300ml/½pt dry white wine
salt and freshly ground
black pepper
dried breadcrumbs for
the mould
1 shallot, finely chopped
¼ tsp saffron strands
2 tsp cornflour

Leeks and mussels are complementary flavours. The rice here unites them and gives substance to this lovely dish.

1 Scrub the mussels in cold water, knock off the barncles and tug off the beard. Rinse in several changes of cold water. Discard any mussel that remains open after you have tapped it against a hard surface.

2 Put the oil, garlic and slice of lemon in a large sauté pan. Add the mussels, cover the pan and cook over high heat until the mussels are open, about 4 minutes. Shake the pan very often.

3 Remove the mussel meat from the shells and discard the shells. Filter the liquid through a sieve lined with muslin. Set aside.

4 Cut off the green part of the leeks. Choose the best green leaves, wash them and blanch in boiling water for 2–3 minutes. Drain and cut into 1cm/½in strips. Set aside.

5 Cut the white part of the leeks into very thin pieces. Wash thoroughly, drain and dry them.

6 Heat the stock in a saucepan until simmering (keep it simmering all through the making of the risotto).

7 Heat the oven to 180°C/350°F/Gas Mark 4.

8 Heat 60g/2oz of the butter and the white part of the leeks in a large heavy-bottomed saucepan. Sauté until the leeks are just soft and then mix in the rice. Sauté the rice until it is well coated with butter and the grains are partly translucent – about 2 minutes – and then pour over half the wine. Boil briskly for 1 minute, stirring constantly.

9 Add a ladleful of the simmering stock and stir well. As soon as nearly all the stock has been absorbed, add another ladleful of stock. Continue cooking the rice in this manner until it is very *al dente*, about 15 minutes. Mix in 30g/1oz of the butter. Taste and check the seasoning.

10 Very generously butter a 1.5l/2½pt cake tin, mould or soufflé dish and coat it with breadcrumbs. Spoon the risotto into it, press down gently and place in the oven while you prepare the sauce.

11 Put the shallot and remaining butter in a saucepan and sauté for 5 minutes.

12 Meanwhile, pound the saffron in a mortar. Add 2–3 tbsp of the mussel liquid and stir thoroughly. Add the cornflour and stir hard until amalgamated. Pour the mixture into the shallot pan and add the remaining wine and mussel liquid. Bring to the boil very slowly, stirring constantly. Allow to simmer for a few minutes for the sauce to thicken and then add the mussels. Add salt and pepper to taste. Cover the pan and draw off the heat.

13 Loosen the risotto from the mould with a palette knife. Turn the mould over onto a heated round platter. Tap and shake the mould and then lift it off. Drape the strips of the green part of the leeks over the risotto at regular intervals. Spoon a little of the mussel sauce over the top and pour the rest into a heated bowl. Serve immediately.

ANELLO DI RISOTTO COI FEGATINI E I FUNGHI

RISOTTO RING WITH CHICKEN LIVERS

AND DRIED PORCINI

Serves 6 as a first course or
4–5 as a main course

For the sauce

30g/1oz dried porcini
30g/1oz unsalted butter
150g/5oz fresh chicken livers
60g/2oz fresh Italian sausage
such as luganega, or Toulouse
sausage, skinned
200g/7oz skinned and boned
chicken breast, cut into
bite-size pieces
100/3½oz podded fresh young
peas, or frozen petits pois
2 pinches of ground cloves
120ml/4fl oz red wine
salt and freshly ground
black pepper

The plain risotto is served in a ring, the centre of which is filled with a rich sauce. It is a showy dish for a dinner party.

1 Soak the dried porcini in very hot water for 30 minutes. Lift them out, rinse them and dry them. Chop them coarsely. Filter the porcini liquid through a sieve lined with muslin.

2 Heat the butter in a small saucepan. Add the porcini and cook gently for about 10 minutes.

3 Meanwhile, clean the chicken livers, removing all the fat and gristle. Cut into bite-size pieces and put in a small saucepan with the sausage, chicken and peas. Add the cloves, wine, and salt and pepper to taste. Bring to the boil and cook, uncovered, for about 10 minutes, stirring very frequently. Mix in the porcini with all their juices and continue cooking for a further 10 minutes. Taste to check the seasoning. Set aside, and reheat before serving.

4 To make the risotto, first bring the stock to a simmer (keep it just simmering all through the cooking of the rice).

5 Heat half the butter with the onion, celery and carrot in a wide heavy-bottomed saucepan. Cook gently until the vegetables are soft, about 10 minutes, stirring very frequently.

6 Heat the oven to 170°C/325°F/Gas Mark 3.

7 Mix the rice into the vegetables and sauté for a minute or so until the grains are partly translucent. Stir in the tomato purée, cook for $\frac{1}{2}$ minute and then pour in the wine. Boil rapidly for 1 minute, stirring constantly.

8 Add a ladleful of the simmering stock and 2–3 tbsp of the porcini liquid. Cook the risotto, gradually adding the remaining stock in the usual way. When the risotto is nearly done and still on the liquid side, draw off the heat. Taste and add salt and pepper. Mix in the rest of the butter and the Parmesan. Cover the pan and leave until the butter has melted, and then mix thoroughly.

9 Meanwhile, generously butter a 1l/1¾pt ring mould. Coat with breadcrumbs, shaking out excess crumbs.

10 Spoon the risotto into the mould. Place the mould in the oven and heat for about 10 minutes.

11 Turn the risotto out onto a heated round platter and spoon the hot sauce into the hole.

For the risotto

60g/2oz unsalted butter
2 tbsp finely chopped onion
1 tbsp finely chopped celery
1 tbsp finely chopped carrot
400g/14oz Italian rice,
preferably Vialone Nano
1 tbsp tomato purée
120ml/4fl oz red wine
1.5l/2½pt chicken stock
salt and freshly ground
black pepper
6 tbsp freshly grated Parmesan
butter and dried breadcrumbs
for the mould

PATATE, RISO E COZZE DI PIETRO

POTATO, RICE AND MUSSEL PIE

Serves 4 as a main course

2kg/4½lb mussels
180ml/6fl oz dry white wine
700g/1½lb waxy potatoes
5 tbsp chopped fresh flat-leaf parsley
3 tsp dried oregano
7 tbsp extra virgin olive oil
1 garlic clove, sliced
salt and freshly ground black pepper
180g/6½oz Italian rice, preferably Vialone Nano
1 large courgette, sliced
200g/7oz Italian or Spanish onion, very finely sliced
5 tbsp grated aged pecorino
400g/14oz Italian canned chopped tomatoes

My friend Pietro Pesce is a serious connoisseur of good food. Being a Venetian, he is also a great champion of northern Italian cooking, so that when he came back from Bari, in the south, and gave me this recipe I was quite sure it was worth testing.

The original recipe advises one not to add the mussel juices to the pie because it would make the dish too salty. But when I tested it with Atlantic mussels, less salty and less flavourful, I decided to add the juices to give the pie the necessary taste of fish and the sea.

---

1 Scrub the mussels in cold water, knock off the barnacles and tug off the beard. Rinse in several changes of cold water until there is no sand at the bottom of the sink. Throw away any mussel which is open and remains open after you tap it on a hard surface. It is dead. Set aside a dozen of the best-looking mussels.

2 Put the wine and the remaining mussels in a large sauté pan. Cook, covered, until the mussels open – about 4 minutes. Shake the pan frequently. Remove the mussels as they open, or they will toughen. Eventually all the shells containing a mussel will indeed open.

3 Take the meat out of the shells and discard the shells. Filter the mussel liquid through a sieve lined with a piece of muslin. You will have about 600ml/1pt of liquid. Set the meat and the liquid aside in separate bowls.

4 Scrub and wash again the shells of the unshelled mussels and set aside.

5 Peel the potatoes and cut them into wafer-thin slices. I use a food processor fitted with the fine blade disc. Put the potatoes in

a bowl and toss them with 1 tbsp of parsley, 1 tsp of oregano, 2 tbsp of the oil, a sliver or two of garlic and a good grinding of pepper.

6 Put the rice in another bowl and the courgette in a third bowl. Dress each of them with 1 tbsp of the oil, 1 tbsp of parsley, 1 tsp oregano, a sliver or two of garlic and a grinding of pepper.

7 Heat the oven to 180°C/350°F/Gas Mark 4.

8 Choose a shallow metal oven dish no more than 5cm/2in deep. Grease it well with some of the remaining oil.

9 Spread the onion over the bottom of the dish and cover with the courgette. Make a layer of half the potatoes and lay all the mussels, shelled and unshelled, over them. Pour about half the mussel liquid into the dish and sprinkle with two-thirds of the cheese. Level down with your hands, then add the rice and cover with the rest of the potatoes. Pour over the rest of the mussel liquid and season with lots of pepper.

10 Spread the tomatoes with all their juice all over the top and add enough boiling water to come nearly level with the top of the pie. Sprinkle with the remaining cheese and parsley and 1 tsp of salt. (Only a little salt is added because the mussel juices and the pecorino should have already salted the dish enough.) Drizzle the rest of the oil all over the pie.

11 Cover the pie with foil and bake for 1 hour. Remove the foil and continue baking until the potatoes are tender, which depends on their quality and on how thin the slices are. Remove from the oven and set the pie aside to rest for 10 minutes before serving, to allow the flavours to blend.

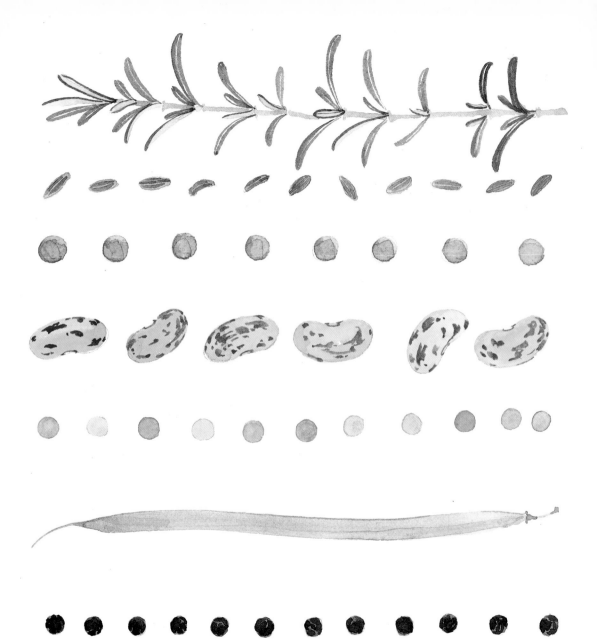

RISI ASCIUTTI E MINESTRE DI RISO

—— RICE AND VEGETABLE DISHES AND RICE SOUPS ——

The first two recipes in this section are for dishes that are midway between a soup and a risotto. The rice is boiled in the stock in which the vegetables are cooking, thus the dishes are definitely not risotti. This method of cooking ensures that the taste of the vegetable predominates over the flavour of the rice.

The last three recipes are for soups, all from my home town, Milan, the motherland of good soups. There, most families start their supper with a soup. Often it is a rice soup, which can vary from a rich earthy minestrone to a sophisticated soup with pieces of chicken and grains of rice and almonds floating in a pale blond pool – a very Chinese looking soup.

RISI E BISI
RICE WITH PEAS

Serves 4–6 as a first course

1 small onion, very finely chopped
45g/1½oz unsalted butter
1 tbsp olive oil
700g/1½lb young fresh peas, podded
1.5l/2½pt light meat stock
250g/9oz Italian rice, preferably Vialone Nano
1 tsp fennel seeds, crushed, or 2 tbsp chopped fresh flat-leaf parsley
75g/2½oz Parmesan, freshly grated
salt and freshly ground black pepper

The Venetians' love of rice and peas is sublimated in this, the most aristocratic of rice dishes. It was served at the Doge's banquets on the feast of San Marco, 25th April, when the first young peas, grown on the islands of the Venetian lagoon, appear in the market.

This is the old recipe, in which fennel seeds are used instead of parsley. The best rice for the dish is Vialone Nano.

1 Put the onion, half the butter and the oil in a heavy-bottomed saucepan and sauté until the onion is pale golden and soft. Mix in the peas and cook over low heat for 10 minutes, adding a few spoonsful of stock during the cooking.

2 Meanwhile, bring the remaining stock to the boil in another saucepan.

3 Add the rice to the peas and sauté for 2 minutes, turning the rice over and over until the grains are partly translucent. Now pour over the boiling stock. Stir well and bring back to the boil. Simmer gently, stirring occasionally, until the rice is *al dente*. You might have to add a little more stock during the cooking.

4 A few minutes before the rice is done, add the fennel seeds or parsley, the rest of the butter and 4 tbsp of Parmesan. Taste and add salt and pepper to your liking. Stir thoroughly and finish the cooking, then serve at once with rest of the cheese handed round separately.

RISO E LENTICCHIE
RICE WITH LENTILS

This is an earthy, nourishing soup which I first had one lunchtime in Rome in a busy, bustling trattoria opposite the Quirinale. It was the most lively place imaginable, crowded with civil servants enjoying good homely Roman food.

1 Heat the oil, onion and pancetta in a heavy-bottomed saucepan. (I use an earthenware pot when I cook pulses.) Sauté for about 7 minutes, stirring frequently. The onion must become soft but not coloured.

2 Chop together finely the carrot, celery, rosemary leaves and garlic. Add to the onion *soffritto* – frying mixture – and cook at low heat for about 10 minutes. Stir frequently. Season with salt and stir in the tomato purée. Cook for a further minute.

3 Meanwhile, heat the stock in a separate saucepan.

4 Add the lentils to the vegetable mixture. Stir well and let them *insaporire* – take up the flavour – for a minute or two.

5 Pour enough stock into the pan to cover the lentils by about 5cm/2in. Place a lid over the saucepan and cook until the lentils are soft, not *al dente*. It is difficult to say how long that will take since it depends on the quality and freshness of the pulses. Usually lentils are ready within 1 hour. Check the liquid every now and then and add more stock whenever the lentils are too dry.

6 Add the rest of the stock and bring back to the boil. Mix in the rice and, if necessary, add more boiling stock. If you have used all the stock, pour in boiling water. The amount of liquid needed varies with the quality of the lentils, the kind of rice used and the heat on which the soup is cooked. The resulting soup should be quite thick: lots of rice and lentils in a little liquid.

Serves 4–5

4 tbsp olive oil
1 small onion, very finely chopped
60g/2oz smoked pancetta, cut into tiny pieces
1 small carrot
1 large celery stick
1 sprig of fresh rosemary, about 5cm/2in long
1 garlic clove
salt and freshly ground black pepper
1 heaped tsp tomato purée
1.5l/2½pt vegetable stock or 2 vegetable stock cubes dissolved in the same amount of water
200g/7oz green lentils, rinsed and drained
200g/7oz Italian rice, preferably Vialone Nano
extra virgin olive oil for the table, a Tuscan or Roman oil

7 Season with lots of pepper, and simmer until the rice is *al dente* (15–20 minutes).

8 Taste and adjust the seasoning. Serve the soup straight away, handing round a bottle of extra virgin olive oil for everyone to pour a little over his serving of soup. Although not essential, I recommend this last *battesimo* – christening – because the oil livens up the earthy soup with its fruity flavour.

RISO CON LE VERDURE

RICE WITH VEGETABLES

Northern and southern Italy meet happily in this dish, which was given to me by the Neapolitan owner of a superb greengrocer in Valtellina, an Alpine valley north of Milan. The dish is halfway between a minestrone and a risotto with vegetables and yet it tastes different from either. The flavour of the vegetables comes through strongly, enhanced by the final *soffritto*.

1 Choose a large pot – I use my earthenware stockpot of 5l/8¾pt capacity. Put all the washed and cut vegetables in it and add enough water to come three-quarters of the way up the side of the pot. Season with salt, bring to the boil and simmer, uncovered, for 45 minutes.

2 Add the rice to the vegetables, stir well and cook for about 15 minutes or until done. The vegetables should be nice and soft and the rice should be *al dente*, thus giving a pleasing contrast of texture.

3 While the rice is cooking, make a little *soffritto* (frying mixture). Heat the oil, garlic and sage in a small frying pan until the sage begins to sizzle and the aroma of the garlic to rise. Add the tomatoes and cook for 5 minutes, stirring occasionally.

4 When the rice is ready, drain the contents of the stockpot very well (you can keep the liquid for a soup) and transfer the rice and vegetable mixture, a ladleful at a time, into a serving bowl. Dress each ladleful with a couple of spoonfuls of the *soffritto*, a handful of cheese cubes, a generous grinding of pepper and a spoonful of Parmesan. Mix very thoroughly after each addition, and serve at once.

Note: By dressing the dish gradually you make sure that the *soffritto* and the cheese are equally distributed.

Serves 6 as a first course or 4 as a main course

1 large waxy potato, diced
2 carrots, diced
1 large leek, white and green part, cut into rounds
120g/4oz podded fresh peas or green beans, according to season
1 celery stalk, stringed and diced
1 courgette, diced
salt and freshly ground black pepper
300g/10oz Italian rice, preferably Vialone Nano
100ml/3½fl oz extra virgin olive oil
3 garlic cloves, finely chopped
12 fresh sage leaves, chopped
2 large ripe tomatoes, peeled, seeded and coarsely chopped
120g/4oz Italian fontina or raclette, diced
6 tbsp freshly grated Parmesan

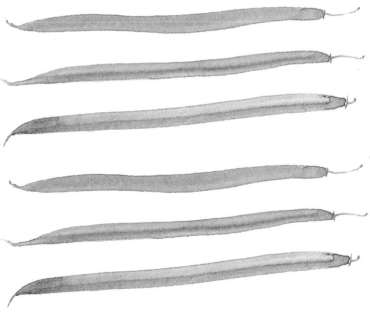

MINESTRA DI RISO, MANDORLE E PREZZEMOLO

RICE, ALMOND AND PARSLEY SOUP

Serves 4

120g/4oz almonds
1.25l/2pt chicken stock
1 chicken breast
120g/4oz Italian rice, preferably Vialone Nano
3 tbsp chopped fresh flat-leaf parsley
salt and freshly ground black pepper

No clear soup like this can be successful without the basis of a good home-made stock. For this recipe I suggest a chicken stock instead of the more usual meat stock.

This is a delicate soup to be given to people who appreciate the balance of good ingredients.

1 Heat the oven to 220°C/425°F/Gas Mark 7.

2 Blanch the almonds in boiling water for 30 seconds. Drain and peel them. Place the almonds on a baking tray and bake for 10 minutes or until the aroma rises and the almonds are quite brown. Chop them to the size of grains of rice.

3 Heat the stock until boiling. Put in the chicken breast and cook gently for 10 minutes. Lift the breast out of the stock and place on a board.

4 Skin and bone the chicken breast. Cut the meat into small strips.

5 Slide the rice into the simmering stock. Simmer for 10 minutes, then stir in the strips of chicken, the parsley and almonds. Cook gently until the rice is *al dente*. Taste and add salt and pepper if necessary, then serve.

MINESTRONE

VEGETABLE SOUP WITH RICE

This is the classic minestrone with rice, or Minestrone alla Milanese, where rice is the starchy nourishment added to a vegetable soup.

1 Heat the oil and butter in a stockpot or a large saucepan, add the pancetta and sauté for 2 minutes. Add the onions, sage and parsley and fry gently for 5 minutes or so.

2 Mix in the garlic, carrots, celery and potatoes and fry for 2 minutes. Add the green beans and courgettes and sauté for a further couple of minutes.

3 Cover with 2.5l/4pt of hot water and add the tomatoes and salt and pepper to taste. Cover the pan and cook at a very low simmer for a minimum of 1½ hours. Minestrone can be cooked for as long as 3 hours and it will be even better. Do not think that the vegetables will break; they do not.

4 About 30 minutes before you want to eat, add the cabbage and cook for 15 minutes. Then add the rice and the canned beans and stir well. Continue cooking uncovered at a steady simmer until the rice is *al dente*. Serve with a bowl of Parmesan on the side.

Minestrone is even better made a day in advance and warmed up. In the summer it is delicious cold, though not straight from the refrigerator.

Serves 6

2 tbsp olive oil
30g/1oz butter
120g/4oz unsmoked pancetta, or unsmoked streaky bacon, chopped
2 onions, coarsely chopped
4 or 5 fresh sage leaves, snipped
1 tbsp chopped fresh flat-leaf parsley
2 garlic cloves, chopped
2 carrots, diced
2 celery sticks, diced
2 potatoes, about 225g/½lb, diced
120/4oz green beans, cut into 2cm/¾in pieces
225g/½lb courgettes, diced
225g/½lb Italian canned plum tomatoes with their juice
salt and freshly ground black pepper
225g/½lb Savoy cabbage, cut into strips
150g/5oz Italian rice, preferably Semifino Padano or Vialone Nano
400g/14oz canned borlotti beans, drained
freshly grated Parmesan, to serve

RIPIENI E INSALATE DI RISO

Two recipes for rice stuffings hardly do justice to an array of dishes in which rice is the primary ingredient of the stuffing. But I have chosen my favourites. While rice is commonly used as a stuffing for vegetables, its use in stuffing fish is less usual. The recipe for squid stuffed with rice is very interesting and very good; in fact, it is my preferred way of stuffing squid.

The versatility of rice is boundless. It even makes excellent salads, which is more than can be said for pasta.

I have also included in this section two of my favourite recipes for rice salads.

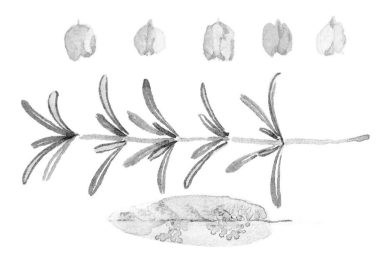

POMODORI RIPIENI DI RISO

—— TOMATOES STUFFED WITH BASIL-FLAVOURED RICE ——

Serves 4 as a first course

450g/1lb ripe tomatoes, all the same size
salt and freshly ground black pepper
90g/3oz Italian rice, preferably Vialone Nano
2 garlic cloves, finely sliced
12 fresh basil leaves, snipped
1 egg
100ml/3½fl oz extra virgin olive oil

The rice in this recipe is not previously cooked, but only soaked in oil so that it retains a stronger flavour. By the end of the cooking the tomatoes are very soft and become amalgamated with the rice, rather than being separate containers.

1 Wash and dry the tomatoes. Cut them across in half. Scoop out some of the seeds and discard. Scoop out all the pulp and the juice with a pointed spoon, taking care not to break the skin. Chop the pulp and put it in a bowl with the juice.

2 Sprinkle the insides of the tomato halves with salt and chill them.

3 Add the rice to the bowl together with the garlic and basil.

4 Beat the egg very lightly and mix thoroughly into the rice mixture. Add the oil, plenty of pepper and salt to taste. Mix again very well and leave for at least 3 hours.

5 Heat the oven to 190°C/375°F/Gas Mark 5.

6 Oil a large oven dish and place the tomato halves in it, cut side up. Fill them with the rice mixture, to come level with the tops of the tomatoes. Cover the dish with foil and bake until the rice is cooked, about 45 minutes. Serve hot.

CALAMARI RIPIENI DI RISO

SQUID STUFFED WITH RICE

Rice, a staple of the north, is sometimes used in fish dishes in Puglia, the heel of the Italian boot. The fish used there for this dish is cuttlefish. Although this is a fairly common species off the south coast of England, most of the best catch there is shipped straight to France and Spain. For this reason I prefer to use squid, which are easily available. Whenever I can I buy the local squid, large specimens with a very good flavour, much better than the small calamari which come from Italy and Spain. These are often frozen or, what is worse, appear to be fresh although in fact they have previously been frozen.

---

1 Ask your fishmonger to clean the squid, or do it yourself by following these instructions. Hold the sac in one hand and pull off the tentacles with the other hand. The contents of the sac will come out too. Cut the tentacles above the eyes. Squeeze out the thin bony beak in the centre of the tentacles. Peel off the skin from the sac and the flap. Remove the translucent backbone from inside the sac and rinse the sac and tentacles under cold water. Keep the sacs whole.

2 Cut the tentacles into small pieces and then chop them coarsely until they are about the same size as the grains of rice.

3 Put 2 tbsp of the oil in a sauté pan. Add the rice, chopped tentacles, parsley, garlic, chilli and lemon zest and sauté briskly for a few minutes to *insaporire* – let the mixture take up all the flavours.

4 Finely chop the anchovy fillets and stir into the mixture. Cook at a lower temperature for a minute or so. Taste and add salt and pepper, if necessary.

5 Heat the oven to 180°C/350°F/Gas Mark 4.

Serves 3–4 as a main course

4 large squid, about 1kg/2¼lb
6 tbsp olive oil
4 level tbsp cooked Italian rice, preferably Vialone Nano
3 tbsp chopped fresh flat-leaf parsley
2 garlic cloves, chopped
½ dried chilli, chopped
grated zest of ½ unwaxed lemon
2 salted anchovies, boned and rinsed, or 4 canned anchovy fillets, drained
salt and freshly ground black pepper
120ml/4fl oz dry white wine

6 Fill each squid sac with the rice mixture. Do not pack the stuffing too tight or the sac will burst during the cooking. Stitch up the opening with a needle and thread and lay the squid in a single layer, close to each other, in an oven dish. (I use a metal tin, because metal transmits the heat better than ceramic.)

7 Pour the rest of the oil and the wine over the squid. Cover the oven dish tightly with a piece of foil and bake for about 1 hour, until the squid are tender when pricked with a fork.

8 When they are done, transfer the squid to a carving board and allow to cool for 10 minutes. Slice off a very thin strip from the sewn end to eliminate the thread. Cut each sac into thick slices of about 2.5cm/1in. If you possess one, use an electric carving knife which will make this slicing very easy. Otherwise see that your knife is very sharp. Gently transfer the slices to a serving dish.

9 Taste the cooking juices. If bland, boil briskly until reduced and full of flavour. Spoon over the squid. You can serve the dish hot, warm or even at room temperature, which I personally prefer.

INSALATA DI RISO CON MOZZARELLA ED ACCIUGHE

RICE SALAD WITH MOZZARELLA AND ANCHOVY
FILLETS

I strongly recommend using buffalo mozzarella for this dish. If possible, dress the rice 2 hours before serving.

1 Cook the rice in plenty of boiling salted water until just *al dente*. (Remember that when served cold, rice is better if a touch undercooked.) Drain the rice, rinse under cold water and drain again. Transfer the rice to a bowl and pat dry with kitchen paper towels. Add 2 tbsp of the oil and set aside to cool.

2 Chop the eggs and add to the rice, together with the mozzarella.

3 Chop the anchovy fillets and place in another bowl. Mix in the parsley, garlic and chilli. Beat in the remaining oil with a fork until the sauce thickens. Season with salt and pepper to taste.

4 Spoon this dressing into the rice and mix very thoroughly with two forks so as to separate all the grains. Taste and adjust the seasoning to your liking. Scatter the olives and capers here and there and serve cold, but not chilled.

Serves 4 as a first course

250g/9oz Italian rice, preferably
Vialone Nano
salt and freshly ground
black pepper
6 tbsp extra virgin olive oil
2 hard-boiled eggs
150g/5oz buffalo mozzarella,
cut into small cubes
6 salted anchovies, boned and
rinsed, or 12 canned anchovy
fillets, drained
4 tbsp chopped fresh flat-leaf
parsley
1 small garlic clove, very finely
chopped
1 small dried chilli, seeded and
crumbled
12 black olives
1 tbsp capers, rinsed and dried

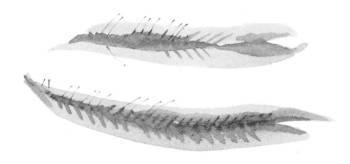

RISO E CECI IN INSALATA

RICE AND CHICK PEA SALAD

Serves 4

150g/5oz dried chick peas
salt and freshly ground
black pepper
1 tsp bicarbonate of soda
1 tbsp flour
1 small onion
1 celery stick
2 sprigs of fresh rosemary
4 fresh sage leaves
a few parsley stalks
2 garlic cloves
7 tbsp extra virgin olive oil
200g/7oz Italian rice,
preferably Vialone Nano or
Semifino Padano
1 garlic clove, finely chopped
a lovely bunch of fresh flat-leaf
parsley, finely chopped
225g/½lb best ripe tomatoes,
peeled and seeded
12 fresh basil leaves, snipped

It is surprising how two ingredients as modest as rice and chick peas can produce, when mixed together, such a really good and attractive dish.

Cook the chick peas properly until they are soft. In common with my compatriots, I find nothing more unpleasant than under-cooked pulses, as they are sometimes served in 'Britalian' restaurants. The rice should be *al dente*, not because of the over-praised 'contrast of texture', but simply because rice is good *al dente*. Chick peas, however, are good when soft.

1 Put the chick peas in a large bowl and cover with plenty of cold water. Mix the salt, bicarbonate of soda and flour with a little cold water to make a paste and stir this into the soaking water. This helps to tenderise the skin as well as the chick peas themselves. Leave to soak for at least 18 hours; 24 is better.

2 Rinse the chick peas and put them in a pot. (An earthenware stockpot is the best for cooking pulses because of earthenware's heat-retaining properties.) Add the onion and celery and cover with water to come about 8cm/3in over the chick peas. Place the pot on the heat.

3 Tie the rosemary, sage, parsley stalks and whole garlic cloves in a small piece of muslin to make a bundle and add to the pot. Bring to the boil, then lower the heat and cook, covered, until the chick peas are ready. The liquid should simmer rather than boil. Chick peas take 2–3 hours to cook. Add salt only when they are nearly done, as the salt tends to make the skin crack and wrinkle.

4 Drain the chick peas (you can keep the liquid for a bean or vegetable soup). Fish out and discard the onion, celery and herb bag. Transfer the chick peas to a bowl and toss, while still hot, with 2 tbsp of the oil.

5 Cook the rice in plenty of boiling salted water. Drain when just *al dente*. Mix into the chick peas.

6 Put the rest of the oil, the chopped garlic and chopped parsley in a small frying pan. Sauté for 2 minutes, stirring constantly.

7 Dice the tomatoes and mix into the *soffritto* – frying mixture. Cook for 1 minute and then spoon over the rice and chick pea mixture. Add the snipped fresh basil and plenty of pepper. Toss thoroughly but lightly. Taste and check the salt. Serve at room temperature.

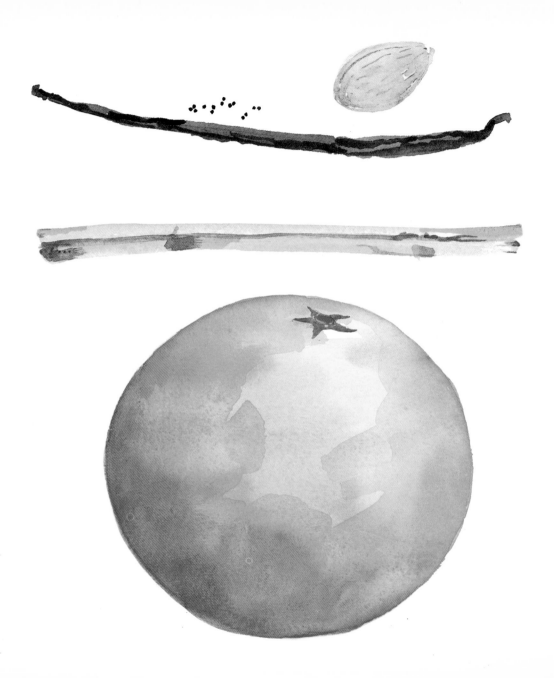

RISI DOLCI

This little book of homage to my home town's staple food ends with three recipes for sweets, although, ironically, they do not come from Milan. The rice cake and rice fritters are from Tuscany and the Black Rice is, oddly enough, from Sicily.

TORTA DI RISO

RICE CAKE WITH ALMONDS AND

SULTANAS

Serves 8

750ml/1¼pt full-fat milk
180g/6oz caster sugar
a strip of unwaxed lemon zest,
yellow part only
a piece of vanilla pod,
2.5cm/1in long
a piece of cinnamon stick,
5cm/2in long
salt
150g/5oz Italian rice,
preferably Arborio
4 tbsp sultanas
2 tbsp dark rum
100g/3½oz almonds, blanched
and peeled (see page 40)
4 eggs, separated
grated zest of ½ unwaxed lemon
butter and dried breadcrumbs
for the tin
icing sugar, to finish

This is the Florentine version of a cake that is popular all over central Italy. I like to make it with Arborio rice, as it swells during the cooking while absorbing the milk. You can add other ingredients according to your taste, for instance chocolate pieces and/or candied peel. What you will have is a firm yet moist cake, not a pudding, that is equally delicious with a dollop or two of thick cream on top or without cream. The cake should not be served until at least the day after making it, to allow the flavours to blend.

1 Put the milk, 30g/1oz of the sugar, the strip of lemon zest, vanilla pod, cinnamon stick and a pinch of salt in a saucepan and bring to the boil. Add the rice and stir well with a wooden spoon. Cook, uncovered, over very low heat for about 35 minutes, stirring frequently, until the rice has absorbed the milk and is soft. Set aside to cool.

2 Heat the oven to 180°C/350°F/Gas Mark 4.

3 Put the sultanas in a bowl and pour over the rum. Leave them to puff up.

4 Spread the almonds on a baking tray and toast them in the oven for about 10 minutes or until they are quite brown. Shake the tray occasionally to prevent them from burning. Cool them a little, then chop them coarsely.

5 Remove the strip of lemon zest, the vanilla pod and cinnamon stick from the rice and spoon the rice into a mixing bowl. (Wash and dry the vanilla pod so that you can use it again.) Incorporate 1 egg yolk at a time into the rice, mixing well after each addition. Add the remaining sugar, the almonds, sultanas with the rum

and the grated lemon zest to the rice and egg mixture and mix everything together thoroughly.

6 Whisk the egg whites until they are stiff, then fold them gently into the rice mixture.

7 Butter a 20cm/8in spring-clip tin. Line the bottom with grease-proof paper and butter the paper. Sprinkle all over with bread-crumbs to coat evenly and shake out excess crumbs.

8 Spoon the rice mixture into the prepared tin. Bake in the oven (still at the same temperature) for about 45 minutes or until a thin skewer or a wooden cocktail stick inserted in the middle of the cake comes out just moist. The cake should also have shrunk from the side of the tin.

9 Leave the cake to cool in the tin, then remove the clipped band and turn the cake over onto a plate. Remove the base of the tin and the lining paper. Place a round serving platter on the cake and turn it over again. Leave for at least 24 hours before serving the cake. Sprinkle with icing sugar before serving.

RISO NERO

BLACK RICE PUDDING

Serves 6

600ml/1pt full-fat milk
75g/2½oz Italian rice, preferably
Vialone Nano
90g/3oz sugar
100g/3½oz almonds, blanched,
peeled and chopped
pinch of salt
pinch of ground cinnamon
150ml/¼pt black coffee
45g/1½oz bitter chocolate,
flaked or grated
grated zest of 1 small orange
15g/½oz unsalted butter
150ml/¼pt whipping cream

There are not many rice dishes in Sicily, but this is one of the few Sicilian contributions to the vast range of Italian rice sweets. It is different from the rice desserts of the central Italian regions – the motherland of rice cakes and puddings – because it contains a high proportion of chocolate and coffee.

In Sicily this dish is served without cream, but even though I am not a cream fan, I must admit that cream lightens the almondy-chocolate flavour of the riso nero.

1 Put the milk, rice, sugar, almonds, salt, cinnamon and coffee in a heavy-bottomed saucepan. Bring to the boil and simmer until the rice is very soft, about 1 hour, stirring frequently. If you use a flame diffuser you can leave it a little longer, but be careful because the milky rice tends to stick to the bottom of the pan.

2 Draw the pan off the heat and mix in the chocolate and the orange zest.

3 Grease a 900ml/1½pt pudding basin with the butter. Spoon in the rice mixture and leave to cool. When cold, cover with cling film and put in the fridge to chill.

4 Free the pudding all round with a palette knife and turn it out onto a round platter.

5 Whip the cream and spread it all over the brown dome just before serving.

FRITTELLE DI RISO

RICE FRITTERS

Serves 4

600ml/1pt full fat milk
pinch of salt
75g/2½oz Italian rice,
preferably Semifino Padano or
Vialone Nano
2 tbsp sugar
pared zest of ½ unwaxed orange,
in strips
pared zest of ½ unwaxed lemon,
in strips
2 size 2 eggs
vegetable oil for frying
icing sugar, to decorate

These fritters are sold and eaten in the streets of Florence as a *merenda*, or snack.

1 Put the milk, salt, rice, sugar and fruit zest in a heavy-bottomed saucepan. Bring slowly to the boil, stirring frequently. Cook, uncovered, at a very low heat for about 1 hour or until the rice has absorbed all the milk and is very soft. Stir frequently. Spoon the mixture into a bowl and allow to cool a little.

2 Lightly beat the eggs to break the white, then incorporate into the rice mixture. Mix very well and place the bowl in the fridge. If possible chill for 1 hour so the mixture firms, which will make it easier to shape and fry.

3 Heat the oil to 170°C/325°F in a wok or a frying pan. At this temperature a piece of stale bread should brown in 50 seconds.

4 Discard the orange and lemon zest from the rice mixture. With a metal spoon pick up some of the rice mixture – a dollop about the size of a large walnut – and with the help of a second spoon slide it into the oil. Fry the fritters in batches until they are golden on both sides. Retrieve them with a fish slice and place on kitchen paper towels to drain.

5 Sprinkle each fritter very generously with sifted icing sugar before serving. They are good hot or cold.

LIST OF RECIPES